ANDERSONVILLE:
A CIVIL WAR TRAGEDY

Linda R. Wade

ROURKE ENTERPRISES, INC.
Vero Beach, FL 32964

Library of Congress Cataloging-in-Publication Data

Wade, Linda R.
  Andersonville: a Civil War tragedy / by Linda R. Wade.
  p. cm. – (Doors to America's past)
  Includes index.

  Summary: Describes the large Confederate prisoner of war camp in Georgia, known as Camp Sumter or Andersonville, and the harsh conditions that killed many prisoners there during the Civil War.
  ISBN 0-86592-472-4
  1. Andersonville Prison – Juvenile literature. 2. United States – History – Civil War, 1861-1865 – Prisoners and prisons, Confederate – Juvenile literature. 3. Andersonville National Historic Site (Ga.) – Juvenile literature. [1. Andersonville Prison. 2. United States – History – Civil War, 1861-1865 – Prisoners and prisons.] I. Title. II. Series: Wade, Linda R. Doors to America's past.
E612.A5W33 1991
973.7'71 – dc20   90-46576
                                                              CIP
                                                               AC

Acknowledgments

      Special thanks to the following people and organizations for information and pictures: Carlene Petty and other staff members of the Andersonville National Historic Site; David Holt, Eastern National Park Association; Gerald Lamby, Drummer Boy Museum; Peggy Sheppard, Andersonville Tourism Director; Ruth Frick, the Trebor Plantation; and Gilbert Young of Huntington, Indiana. He is a Civil War re-enactor on the Union side. He helped me understand what it was like to fight in the Civil War. Thanks also go to Richard Hogue for his editing assistance.

Photo Credits

Courtesy of National Park Service: cover, 1, 5, 11, 16, 24, 29 (right), 30, 35, 37, 40
Andersonville National Historic Site: 10, 12, 15, 17, 19, 20, 22, 26, 29 (left), 32
Linda R. Wade: 39
Andersonville Welcome Center and Museum: 46, 47

Table of Contents

Introduction

Andersonville is the story of a prisoner of war (POW) camp during the Civil War, the bloody struggle between the northern Union and the southern Confederacy. The war took place from 1861 to 1865. There were other military prisons during the war—Camp Douglas and Johnson's Island in the North, and Libby Prison and Belle Isle in the South, to name but a few. In all, between the North and the South, about 60 major prison camps came into existence. But Camp Sumter, better known as Andersonville, was the worst of them all. Located in southwest Georgia, the camp was built in 1864. It was the largest Confederate prison during the war. The camp existed for 14 months.

Like all of the Civil War prison camps, Andersonville was a miserable place. Of the 45,613 Union captives who were imprisoned there, 12,912 of them died from disease, overcrowding, starvation, and exposure to climate and weather. Even for those who survived, existence in the camp was a living death.

Why did so many men die in Andersonville? Who was responsible for the prison's intolerable conditions? What

Indiana Monument located in the Andersonville National Cemetery

happened in Andersonville to earn it finally the reputation for being the Civil War's most notorious and deplorable military camp?

Let's travel to Andersonville. Today the former prison is a well-kept, 475-acre site commemorating the Union men who died there and all of the Civil War dead. Andersonville also stands as a symbol of the horror of all wars. A National Park System Historic Site, it has become a memorial to all Americans who have ever suffered the grim fate of prisoners of war.

1
War and Prisoners

When the Civil War began in 1861, neither side expected a long struggle. Both the southern Rebels and the northern Yankees, as the two sides were often called, believed that the war would end quickly. Neither side considered the idea of holding prisoners or of building prison camps. In fact, few officers had any knowledge or training in how to set up or operate prisoner of war camps.

Early in the war, the governments of the North and South signed the Dix-Hill Cartel. A customary military procedure, the cartel was an agreement that set up the terms of parole and exchange of prisoners. Under parole, a Civil War prisoner signed a promise not to take up arms again. In many instances, the parole was made on the battlefield. The prisoner simply went home. Periodically, the two governments would officially exchange prisoners. The exchange was made on a one-for-one basis, though higher ranked officers had a higher value than soldiers of lower rank. The exchange was simply a swapping of prisoners on paper. The exchange kept the number of prisoners on each side relatively the same, and prisoners never went to prison. Prisons were not necessary under such a system. Parole and exchange also had monetary benefits. The conquering army did not have to provide for the prisoners' needs. The money saved could be used instead to finance the war.

Though the Dix-Hill Cartel was a good idea in theory, it didn't work for long. Some soldiers let themselves be captured so that they could return home to rest or to plant or harvest their crops. Furthermore, keeping records of the numerous exchanges was complicated, and many prisoners violated the parole. In addition, the two sides often could not agree on who to define as a prisoner. Finally, the Federal Secretary of War, Edwin M. Stanton, stopped the exchanges. If prisoners were taken, they would have to be placed in POW camps.

The earliest Confederate camps were near Richmond, Virginia, the capital of the Confederacy. In 1863, however, the camps became a serious drain on Richmond's dwindling food supply. There also existed the constant threat of Union attack, for Virginia was an important Civil War battleground. As prison security became harder to maintain in Richmond, the South realized that it needed prison sites far from the Virginia fields of battle.

Confederate officers chose Andersonville as the site of the new POW camp. Andersonville, a small Georgia community of 20 residents, appeared to be a suitable location. It was close to a railroad, had a creek that provided water, and featured a relatively mild climate. The Confederate army leased land from the local residents and officially named the place Camp Sumter because of its location in Sumter County. Later the prison would be simply called Andersonville.

2

Early Days of Andersonville

In January 1864, Confederate soldiers and slaves from nearby plantations began clearing the land for the Andersonville prison. The original prison would cover 16½ acres of land. It would later be enlarged by 10 more acres. For six weeks, the sound of chopping axes, crashing trees, and burrowing shovels echoed as the sandy soil was stripped of its lofty pines. The logs were cut into 20-foot lengths and hewed by hand so that they would fit closely together. Then the timbers were placed upright in a 5-foot-deep trench to make a stockade fence around the prison pen.

The first 500 Union prisoners arrived at the Andersonville train depot on February 25, 1864. It was two o'clock in the morning. Cold rain fell on the men as they made the quarter-mile trek from the depot to the prison site. They were already soaked from the journey. Union soldiers were transported to Andersonville in cattle cars. Each car would be packed with up to 600 men, standing shoulder to shoulder.

Wet, chilled, and weary they came, many barely able to walk because of war wounds. When they arrived at the

Early days of the prison camp

prison, they found no ready place to sit or lie down. Some finally stretched out in the mud and tried to sleep.

There was no shelter from the weather, and there were no sanitary facilities. Nor had the cookhouse yet been completed. At first, the prisoners' rations—portions of food—consisted of a quart of corn meal, half a pound of raw beef, and a teaspoon of salt. But such meager rations often had to last for days. The absence of a cookhouse and the availability of only a few pots and pans that some prisoners had brought with them made it difficult for the men to prepare what scarce food they had.

Issuing food at the prison camp

The men soon realized that they would have to take care of themselves as best they could, using what items they had with them.

General Richard B. Winder, who had overseen the building of the prison, could not obtain tents. Winder, in charge of all Confederate prison camps, was headquartered in Andersonville because it was the largest camp. His presence there, however, did not make supplies any easier to obtain. Building tools and food items were just as scarce as tents. The increasingly beleaguered Confederacy was using all of its resources to fight the war and

Captain Henry Wirz

feed its own soldiers. Enemy prisoners were not an urgent concern.

In the absence of tents or other housing, the prisoners used their own blankets and overcoats to make little tents that they called shebangs. Other men constructed huts and lean-tos from whatever logs, tree limbs, bushes, shrubs, and brush that were left inside the prison by the construction crew.

At the time the prisoners started arriving in Andersonville, only three prison walls had been completed. Though trees were abundant in the area, the scarcity of tools made logging difficult. The unfinished fourth side of the prison was guarded by artillery. Sentry boxes, which the men called pigeon roosts, were located at 30-yard intervals along the top of the stockade wall. Guards climbed ladders to the pigeon roosts and watched the prisoners. As more prisoners arrived, more pigeon roosts were erected.

Union captives began arriving daily.

Even though the prison was incomplete, as their numbers grew, food rations got smaller, and the wood supply dwindled to nothing. What food there was would be served on an irregular basis, some days not at all.

On March 25, 1864, Captain Henry Wirz arrived at Andersonville to become the commandant, or officer in charge. Born in Switzerland and trained as a doctor, Wirz had come to America and eventually settled in Louisiana where he joined the Confederate forces. He was wounded early in the war. In spite of a lengthy healing period, he never fully recovered before being assigned to Andersonville. He tended to be a rigid and imperious man. The ever-lingering pain of his wound did not soften his disposition, nor did his assignment as commandant. Running Andersonville would be a staggering challenge, for though Wirz would try to operate the prison in an efficient manner, he was faced with ever-dwindling supplies. At the same time, the camp experienced a growing influx of prisoners. Many historians have concluded that, given the existing conditions, running Andersonville would have been an impossible task from the outset – for Wirz or any other man.

3

Life in Andersonville

During the Civil War, being captured and imprisoned was a horror shared by soldiers of both the North and the South. In all of the prisons—Union as well as Confederate—conditions were so bad that survival was considered a miracle. Great numbers of men suffered and died, and the reasons were many. Inadequate medical facilities and personnel, overcrowding, lack of food and shelter, contaminated water, disease, untended war wounds, and the rigors of weather and climate all caused misery and, for many, death.

Sometimes, the deplorable conditions caused prisoners to go insane. There was never much hope that conditions would improve. Both the North and the South were trying to win the war. The proper care of prisoners was far from being a priority on either side. With neither time nor money for the care of enemy prisoners, prisons in both the north and the south were mismanaged. Being in prison was considered to be "the end."

To control the ever-growing prison population at Andersonville, Captain Wirz ordered the construction of a deadline, a row of low posts 3 feet in height, set up 19

Crowded conditions at the prison camp

feet inside the stockade wall. The deadline was intended to prevent escapes by keeping prisoners away from the outer stockade wall. It also reduced trading and talking between the guards and the prisoners. The prisoners would try to trade some of their belongings with the guards in exchange for food. Some guards, eager for a Union trinket or utensil, would make deals. The deadline put an end to such transactions. Guards were ordered to shoot any prisoner who crossed the deadline.

The deadline made prison life miserable for another reason, too. In summer, the tall stockade fence gave some shade from the scorching Georgia sun. But with the

Prison camp in August 1864. Good view of the deadline.

deadline separating the men from the stockade wall, even that tiny bit of shade was lost.

For the first five months of Andersonville's existence, about 400 prisoners arrived daily, making space an even greater problem. The men could barely lie down and stretch out. They each had about the space of a small clothes closet.

Fresh water soon became a problem. A stream, called the Stockade Branch, ran through the prison yard. The stream supplied most of the prison's needs, but by the time it reached the prison yard, it was polluted. The cookhouse was located above the stockade, and the cooks

Conditions were so crowded that the prisoners who arrived later had to put their shebangs near the sinks.

tossed sewage, grease, and garbage into the stream. The water was already polluted from troops stationed upstream. Then, as the number of prisoners in the yard increased, so did their waste, which further contaminated the stream.

The original plan for the prison had called for two dams to be built across the stream. The water in the first dam would be for drinking, and the water in the second dam would be for bathing. The latrines or toilets, called sinks, were to be below the second dam. Flood gates were to be opened twice a day to clean the sinks—but the dams were never built. As a result, the water became contaminated and undrinkable. The smell alone was enough to make men sick. Since the stockade wall was so tall, few breezes entered the prison yard to clear the putrid air. On windy days, neighbors two miles away complained of the odor.

4
Disease and Deprivation

As more and more prisoners entered Andersonville, disease spread. Smallpox, scurvy, dropsy, and diarrhea were but a few of the medical problems. By April 25, three months after Andersonville opened, 2,697 men had been treated and 718 had died.

The first hospital was located inside the prison. However, with limited personnel and medical supplies, it offered little aid to the prisoners. Fresh bandages were not available, so wounds were dressed with dirty cloths. Gangrene became a serious problem because of so much infection. When part of a man's leg or arm was removed, a gangrenous infection usually followed, and the patient often died.

As the prison population grew, food became even more scarce and of poorer quality. Ground corn husks were mixed in with the corn meal, making a course mixture that caused severe diarrhea. Sometimes the men received beans or black-eyed peas and a few ounces of bacon; occasionally, molasses and rice were available. But often the beans were full of insects and the meat spoiled.

Hospital scene

Several prisoners kept diaries during their stay at Andersonville. At times, some wrote in a humorous manner to take the edge off their misery. One man told about the lice, or "gray-backs," as they were called. Millions of lice infested Andersonville. He wrote of having "caught and killed...lice, all fat and in good condition." Talking about "gray-back raising" and "louse fighting," the men joked about the feats of the lice they pretended to be training for exhibition at the next "vermin fair."

If occasional humor helped some of the men keep their sanity, conditions were anything but a laughing matter. The men were always dirty. Soap was in great demand and very short supply. Terrible body odor and dirty clothes were common for the men. Conditions were

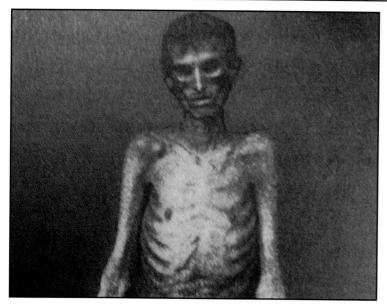

A living prisoner

made even worse because pine was the only wood available for cooking and heating. When pine wood is burned, it gives off a black smoke. The dense smoke filled the air and permeated the men's already filthy clothes.

The hopeless conditions of the prison became unbearable to some sick and wounded men. Such men gave up and threw themselves across the deadline so that the guards would shoot and kill them.

New prisoners often were the first to die. Only those with a powerful desire to live were able to survive. One strong-willed man, John Ransom, kept a diary of all of his prison experiences, including his methods of staying alive. For example, he traded some of his possessions for soap, and started a laundry business, getting paid with precious food rations. Keen ingenuity was all that kept some men alive.

Not all the men were honest. Among the Andersonville prisoners was a group of thieves and ruffians called the Raiders. These social outcasts originally had gone to war to make some money. Further corrupted by the war and prison, they inflicted additional grief on their fellow prisoners. They viciously pounced on anyone who had anything they wanted and became so bold that they robbed and killed during daylight hours, often in plain view.

The Raiders were finally stopped when one victim managed to free himself from these assailants and, with blood streaming down his face, reported the attack to a Confederate sergeant. This time, Captain Wirz came to the gate. As chance had it, he witnessed the Raiders' treachery first-hand. The Raiders were so sure that nothing would be done to them that they committed another robbery right before Wirz's eyes. The angry commandant had the inmates point out all of the Raiders so that they could be rounded up and punished.

At that point, General Winder became involved. He authorized the establishment of a court and trials to be held by the inmates. A jury of 12 men was chosen by lot for each trial. Some Raiders were sentenced to wear balls

Sketch of hanging of the Raiders

and chains; some were set in stocks, wooden frames that confined a prisoner; and others were strung up by their thumbs. Six were found guilty of murder and sentenced to hang.

After the execution, the prisoners formed a police force called the Regulators. From then on, only petty thefts occurred.

5
Despair and Death

Time passed slowly for the prisoners as the cold days of winter gave way to a hot, sultry summer. Temperatures often exceeded 100 degrees. Flies pestered the men; mosquitoes bit them; and, worst of all, the sun burned their weak and abused bodies. Even the shebangs offered little protection. When the humidity rose in the sweltering southern Georgia climate, complete misery descended on the men. The death rate, along with the prison population, mounted during the oppressive summer months. The average number of prisoners as well as the deaths recorded for the summer months were as follows:

Month	Prison Population	Deaths
June	22,291	1,203
July	29,030	1,742
August	32,899	2,993

The largest number of deaths on any one day was 127, occurring on August 23.

But in the midst of August's agony came a reprieve that many prisoners viewed as a miraculous answer to

Providence Spring

their prayers. During a sudden storm, a fresh water spring opened just inside the west deadline. Some men reported that a bolt of lightning had hit the spot; others were not sure. But no one cared how it happened. All that mattered was that the men had good fresh water, pure and continuously flowing. The prisoners called the little fountain Providence Spring, certain that it was a gift of God's divine providence.

With so many men in one place, all professions and trades were represented. Of special comfort to the prisoners were the ministers and missionaries who often used their calling to help the captives. Prayer meetings were held about every other night. At dusk, a song leader would go to a predetermined spot and start singing a familiar hymn. Men gathered around to sing and listen to a preacher. Groups also met on Sunday mornings to study the Bible.

It is hard to imagine how crowded Andersonville prison was. It was originally intended to hold only 10,000 men, but by August its population was more than three times that number. And all the men were crowded into an area of only 26½ acres. That included a broad strip of uninhabitable land in the middle that was so swampy it was called no-man's land. During the summer of 1864, more people lived in that small space than live in many of today's city suburbs.

When a prisoner died, his body was carried to the "Dead House" outside the stockade. Each body was numbered in the hospital register, and an identical number was pinned to the dead man's clothing. If the man's name, company, regiment, and cause of death were known, they, too, were entered in the hospital register.

Burying the dead at Andersonville

Then the body was hauled by wagon to the nearby cemetery. There, prisoners dug shallow burial trenches and placed the bodies in them side by side on their backs. The bodies were buried by number, running from one upward. A total of 12,912 men died and were buried at Andersonville. Each body's number was branded deeply on a wooden stake that was placed above each man's grave.

A prisoner named Dorence Atwater, because of his beautiful penmanship, was chosen to keep the hospital death register. Realizing that one day a list would be needed to notify the relatives of the deceased, he secretly wrote out a duplicate copy of the records. He was afraid the official list would get lost at war's end. Atwater's duplicate list would one day be of great assistance in helping to identify the Andersonville graves.

6

End of the Andersonville Terrors

As summer turned to autumn, the days became a little cooler, bringing some relief to the prisoners. But the greatest relief came when some of the prisoners were moved to other prisons. The Union armies had advanced and were close by in the surrounding states of Tennessee, Alabama, Florida, and the Carolinas, and soon even in Georgia. The Confederates, expecting a raid on Andersonville any day by General Sherman's army, moved a large number of Andersonville prisoners to other camps.

At the same time, many of the 6,000 troops that had guarded the Andersonville prison during the summer were sent instead to fight on the battlefront. Only old men and young boys remained to serve as guards at the prison. Without adequate troops to guard the stockade, Captain Wirz complained of prisoners escaping every night. He recommended that the prison be closed and all remaining prisoners be removed. By the end of November, only 1,359 Union men were still confined in Andersonville.

General Sherman, however, did not march to Andersonville. Instead, he set up headquarters in Savannah. General Winder then removed prisoners from the Carolinas and sent some of them back to Andersonville. The prison, however, was operated on a much smaller basis than originally.

Finally in March, prisoner exchanges were resumed by the North and South. Andersonville prison ceased to exist when the war ended in April, 1865.

Private Dorence Atwater, who had secretly been writing the names and numbers of all the dead prisoners, carried his list in the lining of his coat when he was exchanged in March. He then took the list to the War Department in Washington, believing that families of the Andersonville dead were entitled to know about their sons, husbands, and fathers. The War Department paid Atwater $300 for the list but did not promise to publish it.

In the meantime, however, President Lincoln had contacted Clara Barton. Known as the Angel of the Battlefield, she had been a nurse in Civil War army camps and on battlefields. She would later, in 1881, organize the American Red Cross. Lincoln directed Clara Barton to

Clara Barton at time of Civil War   *Clara Barton raising the United States flag at Andersonville*

determine the location of missing Union soldiers and to notify their relatives.

In August 1865, shortly after arriving at Andersonville, Clara Barton raised the United States flag in the center of the cemetery. Then work began by enclosing the cemetery and identifying the graves of the dead prisoners.

Dorence Atwater had written to Barton, telling her about his list. He then worked with her and a crew of other people to identify and mark the graves in the cemetery. All but 460 of the graves were identified. They were inscribed simply with the words "Unknown U.S. Soldier."

1867 stockade wall

Andersonville was proclaimed a National Cemetery in November 1865, shortly after Clara Barton began her work there. In 1970, Congress authorized the Andersonville National Historic Site to serve as a memorial not just to the men who died in Andersonville, but to all Americans who have ever been held as prisoners of war. In the words of the congressional legislation, the site is "to provide an understanding of the overall prisoner of war story in the Civil War, to interpret the role of prisoner of war camps in history, [and] to commemorate the sacrifice of Americans who lost their lives in such camps."

7
Captain Wirz on Trial

Even before the last Union soldier left Andersonville, word had begun leaking out of the intolerable conditions that existed in the Georgia prison camp. When prisoners began returning home after the war, they angrily confirmed the stories. Northern newspapers published reports of the horrors, and Captain Wirz, as the prison's commandant, was proclaimed the responsible man. Many Northerners put pressure on officials to avenge the disgraceful prison conditions. General Winder probably escaped the same blame only because he died of a heart attack shortly before the war ended.

In May 1865, federal army officials arrived in Andersonville with arrest papers for Wirz. The commandant was then taken to Washington, D.C. where a federal military court tried, convicted, and sentenced him to hang. The charges were that Wirz had conspired with Confederate officials to "impair and injure the health and to destroy the lives...of large numbers of federal prisoners...at Andersonville." He was also charged with "murder, in violation of the laws and customs of war."

Sketch of the Wirz trial

Wirz's legal defense disputed the accusations, but feelings in the North were running high and the court wanted someone to blame for the horrible conditions at Andersonville. Wirz made a convenient and easy target.

The Andersonville commandant was hanged in Washington, D.C. on November 10, 1865. To many Southerners, however, he was, and has remained, a hero and a scapegoat, a man who served his army loyally by doing the best he could in circumstances over which he had no control. For of the countless people involved in the brutal war between the North and the South, Wirz was the only Confederate found guilty and executed for war crimes.

Both sides have given strong defenses of their views. Many Union prisoners proclaimed that Wirz could have provided better food, shelter, medical care, and certainly cleaner water. They claimed that Wirz tried to kill the prisoners simply by neglect.

Others have maintained that there was no conspiracy on the part of Wirz, Winder, or other Confederate leaders to do away deliberately with the federal prisoners. Such researchers point to records that attest to the impoverished Georgia land and the lack of food, medicine, and other necessities of life. The breakdown of the southern economy, they believe, had resulted in extreme shortages. It was that breakdown that was the underlying cause of the horrors of Andersonville.

In a crisis such as war, people often find it convenient and reassuring to have someone or something to blame. At the same time, out of more than 45,000 Union soldiers in Andersonville, nearly 13,000 died. Henry Wirz, the commandant of the prison, was the one accused and executed on the charge of war crimes. Was Wirz guilty? Or was it the conditions of war that were to blame?

8

Remembering Andersonville

After the prison closed, the little village of Andersonville returned to being the simple farming community that it had been before the war. But the train still ran through the town, reminding the residents of the tens of thousands of captives who had passed through on their way to the prison camp.

As time went on, some people in Andersonville believed that greater honor should be paid to the soldiers who died in the prison. Eventually, the Andersonville Guild was formed to restore the town to its Civil War era. And each year after the war, former Andersonville prisoners and their relatives returned to walk the fields and talk of their survival. They wanted Andersonville and those who died there to be remembered.

Back in their home states, the northern veterans and other visitors talked about the prison to their state representatives. As a result, states began erecting monuments in the Andersonville cemetery to honor the men who died in the prison. New Jersey, in 1899, was the first to honor the Andersonville dead with such a monument. Other

New Jersey Monument among the rows of tombstones

states followed: Massachusetts, Ohio, Pennsylvania, Rhode Island, Maine, Michigan, Iowa, Connecticut, Wisconsin, Indiana, New York, Illinois, Tennessee, and Minnesota. In 1976, six years after Andersonville became a National Historic Site, Georgia built a beautiful and touching monument at the cemetery's entrance, honoring all American prisoners of war.

9

A Visit to Andersonville

As you enter the Andersonville National Historic Site, you will find a visitor's center. Be sure to stop by. It contains exhibits on the Andersonville prison, the national cemetery, other Civil War prisons, and the system of paroles and exchanges that was used to deal with prisoners during the Civil War. The center also features videos, tapes, and books that you can use or buy. A stop at the center will add much to your overall appreciation of Andersonville. Especially helpful are the cassettes available for use as you move through the cemetery and prison site. The cassette identifies interesting graves and monuments.

As you approach the cemetery, you'll see a number of monuments positioned throughout the cemetery. These are the monuments built by the states. If you live in the North, try to find the monument built by your state to honor its dead Andersonville soldiers.

One of the first monuments you'll see as you enter the cemetery is the beautiful and solemn Georgia monument. A tribute to all American prisoners of war, it shows three war-torn figures supporting each other.

Georgia Monument with cemetery in the background

As you stand at the entrance of the cemetery and look across the rolling fields of gravestones, you will be astonished by the sheer number of markers. You'll see grave after grave—each displaying an aging marker—row after row, section after section of markers. Today, the Andersonville National Cemetery contains more than 16,000 graves. Of them, 12,912 are of prisoners who died while in Andersonville. The rest of the graves are those of Andersonville prisoners who died later, as well as veterans of other American wars who have been laid to rest in this place of military honor.

The cemetery contains 17 sections. The sections are divided into 4 quadrants that are separated by roads on which visitors can drive. All of the headstones are alike, but Section H contains an unusual marker. It is headstone number 12,196 and marks the grave of L.S. Tuttle. A simply carved, life-size stone dove is attached. Doves are the symbol of peace, but no one knows who placed the dove sculpture there or when or why it was put on that grave. A photo of this headstone is shown on the cover of this book, and represents the peace that now prevails over the area.

After visiting the cemetery, go to the stockade and take a walk across the prison pen where so many men suffered and died. Through the years, grass has grown over the prison yard, making it a grassy field. You'll find it hard to comprehend that nearly 33,000 men lived there at one time. White stakes mark the stockade fence line. Another line of white stakes defines the inner deadline. The central swampy area is still there with the stream, the Stockade Branch, still running alongside it. The men lived on the small hillsides on either side of the swamp.

Providence Spring is marked by a small, open-sided commemorative structure. Water still bubbles up from

Reconstructed prison yard

the same spring that quenched the thirst and gave hope to the desperate men of Andersonville.

One corner of the prison yard has been reconstructed so that visitors can experience the prison yard enclosure. A wall of pine logs and a deadline have been put up, along with several little shebangs. You'll also see the pigeon roosts where guards stood ready to shoot any prisoner who crossed the deadline. As you walk over the prison yard, notice the little holes in the ground. They are the places where the desperate men dug in the hope of

*Water well
escape tunnel*

finding water. Other holes are the remains of tunnels that some men tried to dig to escape from the prison.

Take some time after visiting the cemetery and prison yard to stop and read the markers along the road that winds serenely through the park. The beauty of the landscape will mix with the harshness of war that you have just witnessed. That mix gives a sense that harmony may yet one day prevail among all people of the world.

If you're in Andersonville either at the end of February or in August, you'll have a chance to see two special programs. Those are the times when the Andersonville Historic Site presents two re-enactments of important events in Andersonville's history. At the end of February, there is a re-enactment of the arrival of the first prisoners to Andersonville. In August, you can see a re-enactment of Clara Barton's raising of the U.S. flag in the cemetery after the Civil War. The event is accompanied by marching Union soldiers, a 16-gun salute, and speeches, all delivered in the language of the day. All the re-enactors of these events wear clothes of that period. You'll feel as though you've been transported back into history.

For yet another trip back into Civil War days, take some time to stop by in the little village of Andersonville.

10

The Town of Andersonville

Not far from the Andersonville National Historic Site is the little village of Andersonville. Fewer than 400 people live there today, but they are committed to recreating the town's Civil War era. The village offers a variety of sights to see. Its nicely kept park features an old-time farm, complete with log cabin, barn and farm animals, a sugar cane mill, and a syrup kettle. Sugar cane has been a crop native to the area. Syrup kettles, used to boil sugar cane into molasses, were common in Civil War days. The park also offers pleasant walkways among native trees and shrubbery, giving a quiet feeling of the Old South.

There are two museums in Andersonville that help create a sense of the area's history. One is the Drummer Boy Museum. It contains an assortment of Civil War memorabilia, including watches, pictures, handkerchiefs, uniforms, medical utensils, guns, and letters, to name a few. Don't miss the two drummer boy uniforms—one Union, and one Confederate—complete with drums. The museum got its name from the young drummer boys who served loyally in the armies of both the North and the South. Civil War drummer boys were between the ages of

10 and 15. They tapped their drums on marches and as a summons for retreat. A number of drummer boys, as young as 10 and 12 years of age, and from both the North and South, were taken prisoner along with the older soldiers. There were drummer boy prisoners in Andersonville, too.

Also on display in the Drummer Boy Museum are theater brochures from Washington D.C.'s Ford Theater from the night that President Lincoln was shot there. You can also read pages from the diary of a Union soldier, Captain Albert Wilbur, who served in the same regiment as John Wilkes Booth, the man who assassinated Lincoln. The diary, an excellent source of the history of that era, tells about the assassination and the somber days that followed.

The other museum in Andersonville is located in the town's Welcome Center. The museum contains a variety of items, including farm tools from Civil War days and the dress of Civil War soldiers of both the Union and the Confederacy. It also contains letters having to do with Captain Wirz's trial. Included is a letter written by Wirz's lawyer declaring his belief in Wirz's innocence of war crime charges. You'll also see a special U.S. flag on display: a 35-star flag that flew along the funeral procession route of President Lincoln.

A monument, erected in 1909 and dedicated to Captain Wirz, is located in the center of town. The story of his career and trial is told on the monument's four sides. The monument was built to honor Wirz because many Southerners believe that he was unjustly executed. They believe that if conditions at Andersonville were deplorable, it was because of the extreme shortage of food and supplies, not because of any deliberate plan by Wirz or the Confederacy to cause suffering to the prisoners.

In town you can also see the houses in which Captain Wirz lived and had his office and in which General Winder lived and died shortly before the end of the war.

Try to make time to visit the Trebor Plantation on the outskirts of Andersonville. It will give you a good idea of what life was like before and during the Civil War. It is the only Georgia plantation still in operation that goes back to pre-Civil War days. The name "Trebor" is Robert spelled backwards. Robert is the name of the man who came to own the plantation. Robert Hodges migrated to Sumter County because he held a land grant, family legend says, which he won in a card game. He built what became the largest and most prosperous plantation in the area. His descendants still live there today. During the 14 months that the Andersonville prison was in existence and food was in great demand, wagons of vegetables were sent from the plantation for the prisoners to eat.

The village of Andersonville has two especially important events each year. Though they're both occasions for enjoyment, they are also times that honor those who have died in the service of their country, whether in prison camps or on battlefields. Occasions that recall our war dead remind us of the pain of all warfare.

One event is held on Memorial Day weekend at the end of May. Memorial Day is the day traditionally set aside to honor all those who have died in wars. Inaugurated in 1868, Memorial Day was originally called Decoration Day. Its purpose was to decorate the graves of Civil War veterans. Andersonville's Memorial Day commemorates the war dead, and also offers a weekend of leisure. You can stroll among antique, art, and craft shows.

The town's major event, however, is held on the first weekend of October when the Andersonville Historic Fair brings an explosion of more than 30,000 visitors into the town.

On both Friday and Saturday, a mock Civil War battle is held in the town park. Cannons fire and soldiers run, some acting as though they've been shot, while others

continue to fight. Gunfire and loud booming cannons fill the air with smoke. It's a noisy and solemn event, giving spectators a feeling of what Civil War battles must have been like.

A parade is held on Saturday morning; and all weekend, old-time craftspeople—blacksmiths, potters, glass blowers, quilters, and basket makers—work at their crafts in the town's park. Entertainment includes clog dancers, gunfighters, military bands, gospel singers, and puppets. Men and women—even those coming to attend the fair—dress in clothes similar to those worn in Civil War days.

A stage play, "The Andersonville Trial," is performed on Friday and Saturday at the prison site. The play re-enacts the trial of Captain Wirz, but members of the

Fred and Peggy Sheppard wearing Civil War period clothes

audience are left to decide for themselves whether he was guilty of war crimes or a victim of conditions beyond his control.

A visit to the Andersonville Historic Site and the small town nearby will help you see the price of war as it was paid by those held prisoner there and by all prisoners of war throughout American history. The suffering of such prisoners has always been great, and so is our debt to all Americans who have given their lives in POW camps or on battlefields around the world. Andersonville is a grim reminder of the harshness of war. At the same time, the quiet, moving, and beautiful landscape surrounding it today offers hope that harmony may still prevail among all people.

Index